IMAGES
of Rail

Railroad Depots of Northwest Pennsylvania

This head-on view of the union station at Shenango in Mercer County shows three baggage/freight carts standing at the ready. The station was built by the Atlantic & Great Western Railroad (later Erie Railroad, or Erie) in 1882. The 1919 Erie valuation records say the station was then owned two-thirds by the Erie and one-third by the Bessemer & Lake Erie Railroad (B&LE). B&LE passenger service ended at this station on November 15, 1929. (Courtesy of Steamtown National Historic Site Erie Railroad plate glass negative collection.)

On The Cover: It is a busy day at Butler's Pittsburgh & Western Railroad (P&W, later Baltimore & Ohio, or B&O) station as railroad employees ready baggage for passengers who are waiting for the next train and tend to the appearance of the rails. At the time of this c. 1917 photograph, the Bessemer & Lake Erie Railroad had recently closed its own station and moved its passenger operations here, so the station probably saw an uptick in traffic. This scan is from Interstate Commerce Commission valuation records housed at the National Archives at College Park, Maryland. (Author's collection.)

IMAGES
of Rail

RAILROAD DEPOTS OF NORTHWEST PENNSYLVANIA

Dan West

ARCADIA
PUBLISHING

Copyright © 2020 by Dan West
ISBN 978-1-4671-0577-4

Published by Arcadia Publishing
Charleston, South Carolina

Printed in the United States of America

Library of Congress Control Number: 2020940319

For all general information, please contact Arcadia Publishing:
Telephone 843-853-2070
Fax 843-853-0044
E-mail sales@arcadiapublishing.com
For customer service and orders:
Toll-Free 1-888-313-2665

Visit us on the Internet at www.arcadiapublishing.com

This book is dedicated to my father, Ken West, who was supportive of my depot-hunting hobby and had a keen interest in the old stations.

Contents

ACKNOWLEDGMENTS

Thanks to my good friend Steve Heath for setting off with me one day to look at a railroad station "in the next town over." Once we saw that station, we kept going for years, covering most of Pennsylvania and Ohio and parts of New York. Those trips spawned the online database *Pennsylvania Railroad Stations Past & Present*, which is now over 20 years old, and ultimately led to the publication of this book. Amy Reytar of the National Archives II in College Park, Maryland, provided guidance in using archive resources that saved me a ton of time in locating many of the photographs and records used in writing this book. Stephen Titchenal and his website railsandtrails.com provided expert guidance with Interstate Commerce Commission (ICC) valuation maps and records. My good friend Gus Schulz assisted me at the archive with scanning and research. Scott Woods at the Greenville Railroad Park Museum was generous in providing some great photographs from the museum's archives. Charles Bates of the Allen County Historical Society provided several photographs from their New York Central valuation photograph archives. Richard McKnight of Steamtown National Historic Site was instrumental in helping me find some high-quality photographs from the Erie Railroad plate glass negative collection. My friend Dave Schweingruber and my wife, Jamie West, cast keen proofreading eyes on the text of this book. John T. Slater of the Nickel Plate Road Historical & Technical Society (NKPHTS) provided access to Nickel Plate (NKP) photographs in Erie County. Thanks to the following people for providing photographs, information, tips, connections, and advice during the writing of this book: Mark Barnes, Wayne Cole, Dennis Mead, Ron Stafford, Dan L. Merkel, Gary Moser, Ed Weber III, members of the Railroading in the Mahoning & Shenango Valleys Facebook group, and Jim Cook of Port Allegany. The following archived newspaper sources were invaluable in providing historical information: *Butler Citizen*, *Conneautville Courier*, *Erie Times-News*, *Greenville Record Argus*, and *Newcastle News*. Unless otherwise noted on specific photographs, images are from the author's collection of scans from Interstate Commerce Commission valuation records housed at the National Archives at College Park, Maryland.

INTRODUCTION

No industry in Pennsylvania shaped the economic, social, and industrial fortunes of the state more than the railroads. Following the opening of the Pennsylvania Railroad (PRR) in 1854, the state's coffers of lumber, oil, steel, and coal would soon be unlocked for a greater national market to propel the state to industrial prominence. Within about 30 years, every county in the state had operating railroads, and all but one (Fulton) had some level of passenger service. However, prior to the Pennsylvania Railroad opening, several smaller lines dotted the map.

In Northwest Pennsylvania, the first significant railroad lines were planned and constructed starting in the mid-1840s through the early 1850s. These lines terminated at Erie and ran parallel with the lakeshore, coming into the city from opposite directions. The Erie & Northeast Railroad was constructed between the city and the New York border, where it linked with a railroad from Buffalo. The first Erie & Northeast passenger train reached Erie in January 1852, and by early 1853 had carried over 73,000 passengers. The first passenger station in Erie was built in 1852 by the Erie & Northeast Railroad and was located on the block bordered by Peach Street and Sassafras Street between Fourteenth and Fifteenth Streets (the same site as the two future union stations). Late in 1852, the Franklin Canal Company opened its line between Erie and the Ohio border, where it connected with a line that continued to Cleveland. The inaugural passenger train on those lines ran from Erie to Ashtabula, Ohio, in November 1852. Although these short lines in Ohio, New York, and Pennsylvania would eventually merge to form the Lake Shore & Michigan Southern (LS&MS) Railroad, the width between the rails, or gauge, would become a source of conflict that led to what was known as the "Erie Gauge War." The gauge on the Franklin Canal Company line was 4 feet, 10 inches, whereas the gauge on the Erie & Northeast was 6 feet. To complicate matters further, the gauge of the line in New York to the Pennsylvania border was also 4 feet, 10 inches. Therefore, gauge changes on these lines necessitated inconvenient stops and changeovers at the Pennsylvania–New York state line and in downtown Erie. In 1853, the railroads agreed on a uniform gauge of 4 feet, 10 inches to make the trip from Buffalo to Cleveland and points west a seamless one. Faced with this seemingly positive progress, the citizens of Erie County took the move as an affront to their efforts to make Erie Pennsylvania's only port on the Great Lakes, a center for commerce and shipping. They feared that uninterrupted passage through the county would make Erie just another stop on the line rather than a major shipping port. Their opposition to the uniform gauge took the form of several incidents of mobs tearing up trackage and removing bridges in downtown Erie and at Harborcreek to the east. Mobs so devastated the trackage and bridges that for two months, trains had to stop at Harborcreek, where passengers and freight were transferred to wagons for an overland trip to connect with the railroad again on the west side of Erie. Several more conflicts broke out over the next few years as the matter played out in the courts and via a succession of railroad mergers and agreements. By 1869, the smaller lines from Buffalo to Chicago had coalesced into the Lake Shore & Michigan Southern, with a consistent gauge of four feet, eight and a half inches (now the standard gauge for all railroads). Although the line along the lakeshore was important to the development of transportation in Northwest Pennsylvania in the 1850s, and is still an important double-tracked mainline today, it only represented 46 miles of track.

The next few decades saw several more important rail lines establish a presence in the northwest corner of the state. The Philadelphia & Erie Railroad (P&E), which was in planning stages as early as the 1830s, saw its first passenger train on the full route between its namesake cities in October 1864. From Erie southeastward, the line traversed the Northwest Pennsylvania counties of Warren, McKean, and Elk. Also in 1864, the Erie & Pittsburgh Railroad (E&P) became an important north-south coal-hauling route that operated 83 miles of track from a railroad connection at New Castle (with access to Pittsburgh) to the docks at Erie. Another north-south line in Northwest Pennsylvania was the Allegheny Valley Railroad, which tapped into the oil region of Venango County. Originally planned to run from Pittsburgh to connect with the railroads accessing New York, the line was instead constructed along the Allegheny River to Oil City in 1868, which put it on firm financial footing and enabled it to finally complete its originally planned line from Red Bank in Clarion County to Driftwood in Cameron County in 1874. Yet another railroad key to the development of Northwest Pennsylvania in the 1860s was the Atlantic & Great Western Railroad, which originated in Meadville. Built in fits and starts, the line eventually became part of the Erie Railroad mainline from New York City to Chicago and crossed Northwest Pennsylvania diagonally through the counties of Warren, Erie, Crawford, and Mercer. Other important lines in Northwest Pennsylvania that were started or completed relatively later than the aforementioned lines were the Jamestown, Franklin & Clarion Railroad, which ultimately became part of the Lake Shore and Michigan Southern Railway; the Bessemer & Lake Erie Railroad, which runs from Conneaut, Ohio, to Pittsburgh and through three Northwest Pennsylvania counties; the New York, Chicago & St. Louis (Nickel Plate Road), which parallels the LS&MS lakeshore line through Erie County; the Pittsburgh & Lake Erie Railroad, which was significant to Lawrence County and the city of New Castle; and Baltimore and Ohio Railroad predecessors Pittsburgh & Western and Buffalo, Rochester & Pittsburg, which traversed the southeastern corner of the region. Most of these lines had smaller branches as well, giving this corner of the state a booming network of rail lines handling passengers and freight. This resulted in the construction of hundreds of passenger and freight stations in the largest cities of the region as well as the smallest towns. Due to mergers, acquisitions, fires, floods, and the passage of time, many of the cities and towns had multiple generations of stations.

Through old photographs (and a few newer ones), this book gives a sampling of some of those passenger and freight stations that became hubs of economic activity and important departure and arrival points for passengers.

One

Erie and Crawford Counties

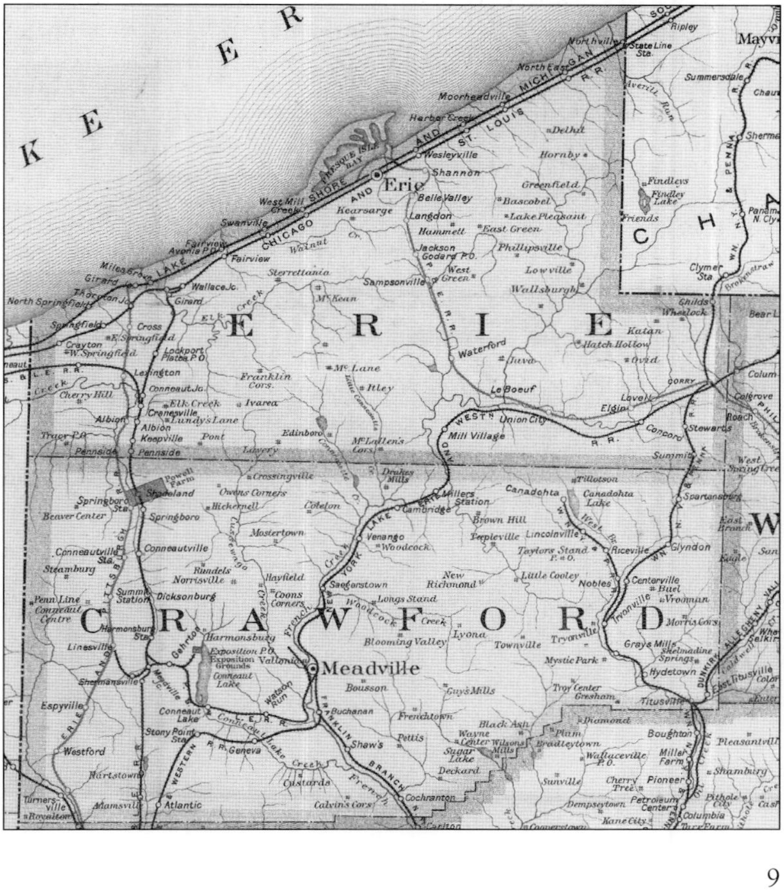

The counties of Erie and Crawford hosted three mainlines. The New York, Chicago & St. Louis, Lake Shore & Michigan Southern, and Atlantic and Great Western gave residents access to major cities in the East and Midwest. Although the major regional lines Erie & Pittsburgh Railroad and Philadelphia & Erie Railroad (later PRR) never reached their namesake cities from Erie with their own trackage, they were major local thoroughfares.

Erie's first Union Depot was built on the site of the old Erie & Northeast Railroad (later LS&MS) station at a cost of $100,000 in 1865–1866. The station was built by two LS&MS predecessors, but also served the Philadelphia & Erie (later PRR) and Erie & Pittsburgh (also later PRR). The Romanesque Revival–style station featured male and female waiting rooms, offices, and a nearly 100-foot-long dining hall.

Erie's second Union Depot was built in 1927 at a cost of $1.5 million. Built by the New York Central Railroad (NYC), it also served the Pennsylvania Railroad. It was the first Art Deco–style station in the United States. Today, the station serves as a corporate headquarters, houses a brewpub, and is an Amtrak stop for the Lake Shore Limited. This photograph was taken in 2012. (Photograph by Ron Stafford.)

The New York, Chicago & St. Louis Railroad (more commonly known as the Nickel Plate) built these twin station buildings in Erie in 1882. The building on the right was the passenger station, and the building on the left was the baggage room and storage area. In the 1960s, after passenger service ended, the buildings were both used as freight stations.

The Nickel Plate freight station in Erie was just down the tracks from the twin passenger station buildings at the German Street crossing. In this 1918 valuation photograph, the station platform appears to need a bit of tidying as it seems to be loaded with junk. Two switch stands are also seen leaning against the side of the two-story headhouse.

The redbrick freight station of the Lake Shore & Michigan Southern Railroad (later NYC) on Sassafras Street in Erie was built in 1905. It covered the length of a city block with a 500-foot-long shed section and featured 52 loading doors on the north and south sides. At the time of its construction, it was heralded as one of the sturdiest on the system with reinforced maple floors and a 12,500-pound Buffalo scale. The photograph above shows the station in 1918. Given its sturdy construction, it still stands today and is seen largely unchanged in the 2000 image below in its current incarnation as a warehouse for a moving company. (Below, photograph by Steve Heath.)

The August 1937 photograph above shows the Bessemer & Lake Erie passenger and freight stations in Erie. These were terminal-type stations with the tracks ending just to the right of the frame. This was the lone track at the passenger station, so the view of the driveway is actually of the passenger boarding area as well. The brick passenger station was built in 1898, replacing the original 1891 wood frame station. The first freight station was one-story and opened in 1893. It was extended in length in 1903. At some point between 1917 and 1921, a two-story head end was added, as shown below in the January 1945 image that looks east on West Twelfth Street toward Peach Street. (Both, courtesy of Greenville Railroad Park & Museum.)

Pictured here are the stations at Harborcreek for the Lake Shore & Michigan Southern Railroad (above) and the Nickel Plate Road (below). The two stations were on the same street a short distance from each other as the two railroad lines run parallel through the area. The northeast corner of Erie County had the largest concentration of Concord grape farms in the United States as well as healthy crops of melons, sour cherries, and peaches. In the photograph below, a farmer is shown bringing a wagonload of fruit to the Nickel Plate station to load onto a climate-controlled Fruit Growers Express boxcar. (Below, courtesy of the Nickel Plate Road Historical & Technical Society.)

Wallace Junction, on the north side of Girard, was a joint station for the Nickel Plate and Bessemer & Lake Erie Railroads. B&LE trains could then access Erie to the east via trackage rights on the Nickel Plate. Once in Erie, the B&LE had its own tracks from a place called Cascade (named after the creek that flows there) to its own terminal station. (Courtesy of the NKPHTS.)

Although the village of West Springfield did not have a railroad running directly through town, it was served by two stations. Crayton Station, shown here in 1936, served the town on the Nickel Plate Road a couple miles to the north. There was also a West Springfield station on the Bessemer & Lake Erie Railroad's Conneaut Branch southeast of town. (Courtesy of the NKPHTS.)

North Springfield's station on the Lake Shore & Michigan Southern Railroad likely dated to around 1852 when the line opened. Located just west of Crooked Creek, the site also featured two water tanks and an engine house in the late 1800s. The station is seen here in 2000, long after it had been repurposed for farm use. It has since been torn down. (Photograph by Steve Heath.)

In 1893, Girard was one of only 10 station stops for the six daily express trains between Buffalo and Chicago on the Nickel Plate Road. The station, shown here in 1976, was eventually cut in two pieces and moved about a mile from its original location, where it sits restored today. (Photograph by Howard Ameling, courtesy of the NKPHTS.)

The Lake Shore & Michigan Southern Railroad station at Fairview was also used by the Erie & Pittsburgh Railroad, as the latter had trackage rights along the line to have access from its northern terminus just west of Lake City at Girard Junction east to Erie. According to railroad valuation records, this station was built in 1913, so it was not the first depot at Fairview.

Similar to many of the towns along the lakeshore, the mainlines of the Lake Shore & Michigan Southern Railroad and the Nickel Plate Road ran parallel and were a short distance from each other. The modest station at Wesleyville, just east of Erie, was little more than a passenger waiting shelter shared by the two railroads. (Courtesy of the Nickel Plate Road Historical & Technical Society.)

Moorheads, between Harborcreek and North East, had stations on both the Lake Shore & Michigan Southern Railroad and the Nickel Plate. As the two main lines paralleled each other here and were only 30 yards apart, the stations could be seen from each other. The stations served little more than a collection of farms mostly owned by the Moorhead family and their descendants, hence the station's name. Fourteen Moorhead families lived around the station in the early years of the LS&MS railroad, hence the smaller station (pictured above in 1919). By the time the Nickel Plate station pictured below was built around 1881, the town had grown a bit more and called for a larger structure. (Above, courtesy of Allen County Museum & Historical Society collection; below, courtesy of the NKPHTS.)

Above is the second Lake Shore & Michigan Southern Railroad station at North East. It was built in 1869 to replace the first station there and served as both a passenger and freight station. It was moved 400 feet down the tracks when the LS&MS built a new brick passenger station in 1899 (below). After the wooden station was moved, it served as a freight-only station until 1957. The freight station was between two large canning operations: the Welch Grape Juice Company and the North East Preserving Company, which can be seen at left above. The brick passenger station was retired by the New York Central in 1960. Both stations still stand as part of the Lake Shore Railway Museum complex, which features several locomotives, passenger cars, and rolling stock on the grounds.

The Nickel Plate had a more modest presence at North East than the Lake Shore & Michigan Southern with this wood-frame passenger station pictured in the 1950s. A freight station across the tracks handled the big grape shipments every year. In 1893, the Nickel Plate shipped 136 carloads of grapes, while the LS&MS shipped 392 carloads. (Courtesy of the Nickel Plate Road Historical & Technical Society.)

The Lake Shore & Michigan Southern station at Swanville, shown here around 1916, was the first station west of Erie. It was of typical early 1870s design with a deluxe outhouse addition. Pennsylvania Railroad timetables from the late 1800s for the Erie & Pittsburgh Division also list this as a station, as the PRR had trackage rights on the LS&MS lakeshore line from Girard into Erie.

According to Erie Railroad records, the station at Cochranton was built in 1876. The railroad arrived in 1863 from Franklin, so this may have been the second depot here. The station was cut in two and moved to the Cochranton Community Fairground in 1984. It still stands and has been restored. (Courtesy of Steamtown National Historic Site Erie Railroad plate glass negative collection.)

Meadville was established as a central point of importance from the start of the Atlantic & Great Western Railroad. The railroad opened this Carpenter Gothic–style station featuring a 327-by-130-foot train shed soon after its arrival in 1862. The depot complex, called "the most complete and magnificent railroad station in America" by the *Pittsburgh Post* in 1863, housed the railroad's general offices, ornate waiting rooms, and an adjacent hotel.

Despite longtime Meadville residents' affinity for the old station, the Erie Railroad erected this redbrick structure in 1893 as a replacement; soon into its construction, according to the *Meadville Evening Republican*, it found favor with the locals. Although part of the old wooden hotel was still attached to it for many years, it was eventually removed and supplanted with a park. Efforts to beautify adjacent Mead Park escalated in 1914 with the installation of a fountain, with the sculpture facing the tracks to serve as a welcome rest area for travelers. At various times, the fountain featured goldfish that were donated by local residents or trout that were sent from the Corry State Fish Hatchery. The park was razed in the early 1970s and is now the site of the Downtown Mall parking lot.

In 1912–1914, the Erie Railroad double-tracked the line between Meadville and Corry to eliminate steep grades and increase traffic. Several stations along the line were either moved or replaced. When the new line went into operation, the Saegertown station was still in its original location with a boxcar body and platform serving as a temporary station on the new highline. Two years later, the station was moved from its original location to the new track, which was 12 feet above the old grade. Originally built in 1872, the station was given a thorough remodel and stucco facelift when it was moved, but the distinctive cupola in the middle remained. The photograph above shows the station before the move, and the image below shows it after the move and remodel.

Millers was a very small town with two stations for the same railroad. The original station, with its freight house made of two converted boxcars, is pictured above. It served the small town, which once included a hotel, store, church, and blacksmith shop. During the double-tracking project between Meadville and Corry in 1913, the Erie Railroad built a new station on the highline, pictured below. The two stations, the old one serving westbound trains and the new one serving eastbound trains, were connected by a driveway. Both stations and the highline track are long gone, but the driveway that cuts up the hill through the woods is still accessible. (Above, courtesy of Steamtown National Historic Site Erie Railroad plate glass negative collection.)

Seen above, the Atlantic & Great Western station at Mill Village was built in 1864 shortly after the tracks were laid through the area. In 1913, when the railroad completed the double-tracking project between Meadville and Corry, this became the westbound station, and another depot (below) was installed on the new eastbound track, similar to the arrangement at Millers Station. In 1915, the borough filed a complaint with the Pennsylvania Public Service Commission against the railroad asking for more trains to stop here because passengers could not travel eastbound and return the same day due to only one train stopping each day in each direction. The resulting order favored the borough, calling for two trains stopping in each direction in the morning and afternoon. (Below, courtesy of Fort LeBoeuf Historical Society.)

Atlantic, on the Erie Railroad, was only a little over a mile west of Adamsville. In fact, Atlantic was originally known as Adamsville Station, but the name was changed to honor the railroad (the Atlantic & Great Western at the time of the change). (Courtesy of Steamtown National Historic Site Erie Railroad plate glass negative collection.)

The Erie Railroad station at Geneva was fairly quiet until the construction of the Keystone Ordnance Works TNT factory in 1941. Much of the initial materials for the construction of the plant arrived at this depot. A nearby spur is still active, but the ordnance works and the station are long gone. (Courtesy of Steamtown National Historic Site Erie Railroad plate glass negative collection.)

When Corry's Union Station was built in 1866, it served the Erie Railroad, Philadelphia & Erie Railroad, and the Oil Creek Railroad (later also part of the PRR). The Oil Creek Railroad (OCRR) was originally a six-foot wide-gauge line. Around the time of the depot opening, the OCRR added a standard gauge rail to the line so it could connect with the P&E. The Erie and OCRR tracks were on the south side of the station, and the P&E tracks were on the north. In the late 1800s, two large hotels were near the station with the Union Depot Hotel between the tracks just a few feet from the station. (Below, courtesy of Steamtown National Historic Site Erie Railroad plate glass negative collection.)

Both the Erie and Pennsylvania Railroads had significant freight stations in Corry with two-story head house offices and long platforms. Because the freight houses were between the tracks of the two railroads, this made freight transfer operations easy. Shown here is the Erie Railroad freight station. The Pennsylvania freight station was just a few hundred feet to the west.

Corry began petitioning the railroads for a new station beginning in the early 1900s. Both the Erie and Pennsylvania Railroads deferred, citing unfavorable economic conditions, for almost a half-century until this new brick station was finally built there by the Erie Railroad in 1952. This utilitarian station and its nearby companion brick freight house still stand today, seen here in 2000. (Photograph by Steve Heath.)

According to Erie Railroad records, the second passenger station at Union City, shown above, was built in 1871, replacing an earlier station that was built around 1862 on the same site. In 1871, the railroad wanted the station to be placed at the junction of the Erie (at the time the Atlantic & Great Western) and the Union & Titusville Railroad, which crossed about a half-mile east of the original station site. Businesses near the original depot lobbied to keep the station close to the business district. Business owners got their wish, and the station site remained the same. The freight station, similar to the design at Corry, is shown below. (Both, courtesy of Steamtown National Historic Site Erie Railroad plate glass negative collection.)

The Erie Railroad station at Cambridge Springs was built in 1891, remodeled in 1914, and torn down in 1964. The current Cambridge Springs fire station now sits on the old Erie station property. The land for the fire station was donated to the borough by the Erie-Lackawanna Railroad with the stipulation that the fire station contain a waiting room for passengers. Passenger service on the line had dwindled by then, so a full railroad station was not needed, and it is not clear if the fire station was ever used for a passenger waiting room. Both images here, above from around 1916 and below from around 1909, show evidence of a brisk passenger business during that era. (Below, courtesy of Steamtown National Historic Site Erie Railroad plate glass negative collection.)

The Erie Railroad station at Concord had a unique look because it was both a tower and a control station. On the night of August 12, 1904, a meteor struck near the station and, according to the *Erie Times-News*, caused an explosion and high wind lasting 15 seconds. Telegraph lines malfunctioned, but the station was unharmed. (Courtesy of Steamtown National Historic Site Erie Railroad plate glass negative collection.)

The depot at Venango was built in 1881, replacing the previous station that burned down two years prior. The station was on the east bank of French Creek, and the borough is on the west bank. The access bridge and the station are both gone, but one set of tracks remains. (Courtesy of Steamtown National Historic Site Erie Railroad plate glass negative collection.)

The Dicksonburg, Bessemer & Lake Erie station predated the railroad, as its original use was as a schoolhouse. After that, it served as a residence before it was purchased by the railroad in 1891 and moved trackside. The view above shows the station a short time before it burned down on July 4, 1916. The cause of the fire was one common to stations: sparks from a passing locomotive ignited the roof. There was a permanent sign on the side of the station announcing events at Exposition Park at Conneaut Lake. The photograph below is a 1941 view of the new station the railroad built as a replacement soon after the old station burned. (Below, courtesy of Greenville Railroad Park & Museum.)

The Bessemer & Lake Erie station at Albion was at the south end of the classification yard there. The complex was originally built in 1891, with the yard being expanded and improved in the early 1900s. It was at Albion's 3,000-car capacity yard where trains from Conneaut, Ohio, and Erie were received, and coal and iron ore trains were assembled. (Courtesy of Greenville Railroad Park & Museum.)

The Conneaut Lake station on the Bessemer & Lake Erie line was one of the oldest depots on the railroad. The station was originally built by the Meadville Railway in 1881, ten years before the line became part of the Bessemer. The depot was on the south side of Conneaut Lake and was torn down in the late 1970s. This image was captured in 1941. (Courtesy of Greenville Railroad Park & Museum.)

The Bessemer & Lake Erie depot at Meadville dates to the original Meadville Railway in 1881. The Erie & Pennsylvania Railroad also used this station from 1881 to 1884 with trackage rights from Linesville. The station housed Meadville Farm & Garden from 1969 to 2019 and now houses the French Creek Valley Railroad Historical Society. The building, seen here in 1999, is in the process of being converted into a museum and community center. (Author photograph.)

Meadville Junction is where the Bessemer & Lake Erie Railroad crossed the original Meadville and Linesville Railroad. The station, which included a lunchroom, was built in 1892 when the original Bessemer line was built through here from Osgood heading toward Albion. The station was closed to passenger traffic one month after this photograph was taken in August 1935. (Courtesy of Greenville Railroad Park & Museum.)

Shadeland, just north of Springboro on the Bessemer & Lake Erie Railroad, was outfitted with a collection of small buildings, including a passenger shelter, small freight house, tool house, and an outhouse. In the late 1800s, the nearby Powell Brothers farm put on horse shows for excursion trains that would stop at the station for the entertainment of passengers. This photograph was taken in 1931. (Courtesy of Greenville Railroad Park & Museum.)

This 1939 view of the double-tracked Bessemer & Lake Erie Railroad at Adamsville shows the 1891 depot on the right. Prior to the arrival of the railroad, the depot site was occupied by a lock on the Erie Extension Canal. All that remains today is a single track and the collapsed remnants of the building on the left. (Courtesy of Greenville Railroad Park & Museum.)

When the Pittsburgh, Shenango & Lake Erie (later B&LE) laid tracks along the old canal towpath through Conneautville, the citizens ponied up $3,000 in subscription fees to help fund the brick station pictured above. When the depot was completed in 1891, the *Conneautville Courier* urged "those in arrears [to] pay up promptly that the promises of our citizens be made good." The Conneautville, Erie & Pittsburgh station, pictured below, was almost two miles from the center of town to the west. This distance meant a lucrative business for H. Everett's Hack Line, which offered service to and from the depot to meet all trains. Inclement weather often meant that road conditions were less than ideal, but Everett's line had a reputation throughout the late 1800s for being on time.

Espyville Station on the Erie & Pittsburgh Railroad was about a mile and a half east of Espyville proper. The old railroad grade at Espyville Station can still be seen, but not much else remains, save for a few houses. Built in 1890 after the previous depot burned in December 1889, the new station was described in the *Conneautville Courier* as "a very tasty building, a credit to our place and the railroad company."

The Erie & Pittsburgh Railroad station at Linesville was also used by the Bessemer & Lake Erie since the Meadville & Linesville branch of the B&LE ended near the station. The joint use of the station began in 1901. In the 1880s, the Erie & Pittsburgh train going south from Erie met the train going north from Pittsburgh at Linesville each evening at 6:00 p.m.

Spartansburg was an early station on the Oil Creek and Allegheny River Railroad. Later, that railroad became part of the Western New York & Pennsylvania (WNY&P, later part of the PRR). The station began its years of service at the east end of the business district on Main Street, as shown in the photograph above. When the Pennsylvania Railroad lowered the grade of the tracks in 1913 during a rerouting of the line, the station was moved a couple blocks north, where it is shown in the photograph below. The tracks formerly ran from Spartansburg to Corry on the east side of Clear Lake. The new cutoff went along the west side of the lake up through Lovell. It was a more circuitous route to Corry, but it had a much lower grade and required less engine power for freight trains.

The Western New York & Pennsylvania is shown at Tryonville in this 1967 photograph. This was the beginning of the "Pigtail" branch (formerly the Union & Titusville Railroad) that went north to Canadohta Lake. In the early 1900s, two trains per day went from Tryonville to the lake. The station was abandoned and stood until it collapsed in the early 2000s. (Photograph by Ed Weber III.)

There were originally two stations at Centerville. One was on the Oil Creek & Allegheny River Railroad (OC&AR) mainline on the east side of town, and the other was on the OC&AR Union Branch on the west side of town. The station on the Union Branch was gone by 1897, and the other was replaced by the Pennsylvania Railroad station pictured here. It was demolished in a May 28, 1951, derailment.

The Titusville Pennsylvania Railroad depot was constructed by predecessor line Oil Creek & Allegheny River Railroad in 1870–1871. In its heyday, 12 passenger trains per day stopped here. The *Titusville Herald* reported that newlyweds so frequently boarded the trains for Niagara Falls here in the summer months that the platform was littered with rice almost daily. The station was torn down in 1964.

The Dunkirk, Allegheny Valley & Pittsburgh Railroad (later NYC) station at Titusville is shown in the aftermath of the 1892 Oil Creek Flood that was, at the time, compared to the Johnstown flood of 1889. Although not as large in scope as the more famous disaster, the horrors visited upon Titusville after a dam upstream collapsed, sending an oil-covered and burning wall of water south, were comparable. Seventy-five Titusvillians lost their lives.

Two

Mercer and Lawrence Counties

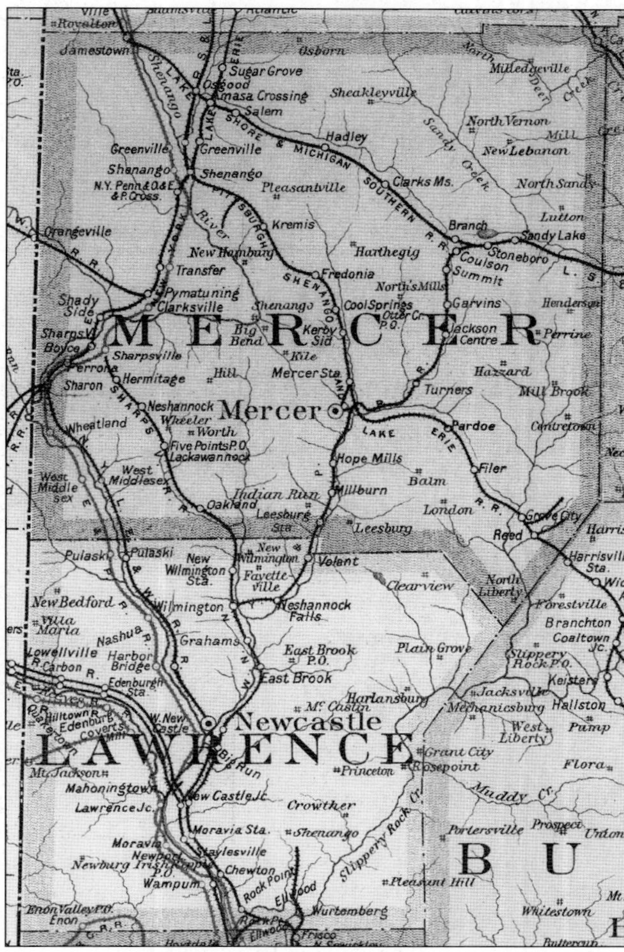

Mercer and Lawrence Counties are known for the past industrial glory of Greenville and New Castle. Greenville was the heart of the Bessemer & Lake Erie Railroad and hosted its car shops from 1893 through 2004. New Castle was once the home of the largest tin plate mill in the United States and was situated along several important railroad lines running from Pittsburgh to Youngstown.

Pictured above is the second permanent Atlantic & Great Western station at Greenville. It opened in October 1872 and also served as the station for the Shenango & Allegheny Railroad (later B&LE) prior to that line building a station in town. The station was extensively renovated in 1954 with new doors, windows, brickwork, and paint. Passenger service ended in 1970, and the depot still stands and is used by railroad maintenance crews. On the other side of the tracks from the passenger station was the Erie freight station, which is shown below. It was built at the same time as the passenger station. It fell into disrepair after being vacated in 1976 and was demolished by Conrail on June 29, 1981.

The Shenango union station was the second large station on the mainline in the Greenville area as it was a mere two miles southwest of the Greenville station. The Erie & Pittsburgh Railroad had a similar arrangement with its stations at Greenville and Shenango. The above photograph shows the Erie Railroad side of the station while the photograph below shows the Bessemer & Lake Erie side with that company's distinctively-lettered signboard. This photograph also shows entrances for the lunchroom and the Wells Fargo Express office. The signboard places the station 65 miles from Erie and 56 miles from Butler on the line. No stations are left at Shenango now, and the area where the stations used to be is not even accessible by road. (Both, courtesy of Steamtown National Historic Site Erie Railroad plate glass negative collection.)

"Transfer" was the functional name given to this joint Erie/PRR station between Greenville and Sharon. In the 1860s, the predecessor roads Atlantic & Great Western and Erie & Pittsburgh had different gauge tracks, so the station was established to transfer freight between the two lines. (Courtesy of Steamtown National Historic Site Erie Railroad plate glass negative collection.)

The village of Orangeville is in Ohio, but its depot was on the east side of the county road that followed the state line, putting it in South Pymatuning Township in Mercer County. The station was on the Youngstown cutoff line, which diverged from the mainline at Transfer and reconnected at Leavittsburg, Ohio. (Courtesy of Steamtown National Historic Site Erie Railroad plate glass negative collection.)

The Erie Railroad had a unique depot at Sharon. This passenger station was formerly two separate buildings that had previously served as a dry goods store. The railroad simply added a canopy along the side and converted the building into a station in 1888. While it served as a station, the railroad rented part of the first floor to a grocery store and leased apartments on the second. Passengers had to cross the street to get from the station to board the trains. Later, this building was replaced with a fully brick structure that still stands today and served the Erie Railroad through the end of passenger service. (Below, courtesy of Steamtown National Historic Site Erie Railroad plate glass negative collection.)

This shared Erie Railroad/Pittsburgh & Lake Erie Railroad freight house was on the west side of South Dock Street in downtown Sharon. According to Erie Railroad records, the station was built in 1911. The Pittsburgh & Lake Erie accessed Sharon via trackage rights over the Erie's Ferrona Branch, which ran from New Castle to the Ferrona Yard on the north side of Sharon.

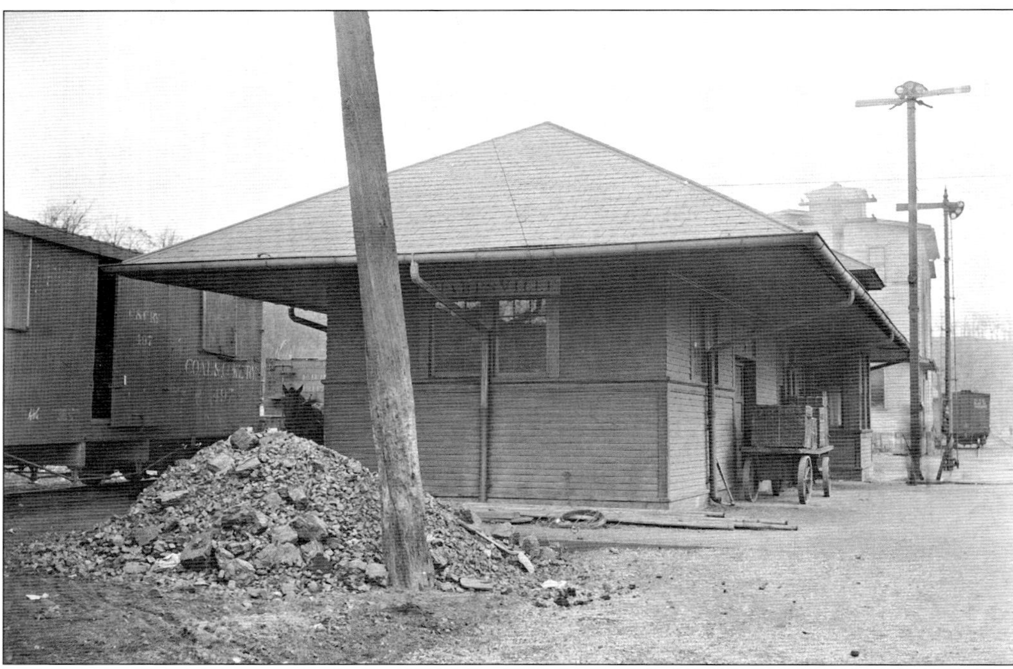

The Erie Railroad originally took a winding path through Sharpsville along the Shenango River in order to reach some of the nine blast furnaces the borough once boasted. The station is gone, but the former Sharpsville Flour Mill, visible in the background, still stands today. (Courtesy of Steamtown National Historic Site Erie Railroad plate glass negative collection.)

The Sharpsville Erie & Pittsburgh Railroad station is seen here looking east from Walnut Street with the old Big Cut Bridge in the background. The Sharpsville Railroad (SRR) crossed the Erie & Pittsburgh Railroad under this bridge. This crossing was needed by the SRR, but the E&P protested the crossing, ultimately losing in court. Just out of frame to the left was the small SRR station.

The Pulaski, Erie & Pennsylvania Railroad (later PRR) station pictured here was built in 1888. The railroad opened through Pulaski in the mid-1860s, so this was likely the second station here. The railroad and the station were along the west side of the Shenango River, with the town and the Erie Railroad on the east side.

The Wheatland depot on the Erie & Pittsburgh Railroad (above) dates to the early 1870s, as evidenced by its simple profile. In 1918, when the Pennsylvania Railroad made Wheatland the division point between Pittsburgh and Erie, a roundhouse, coal tipple, water tank, repair shops, and new switches were added near the station. Rather than building a new station, the railroad simply moved the old station to accommodate the improvements. Farrell's E&P (later PRR) station (below) was only about a mile north of the Wheatland depot. The railroad invested in a new brick station here in 1901 to coincide with the building of the Sharon Steel Mill. The station was actually inside the mill gates to serve the commuting workers. Farrell was known as South Sharon until 1912.

The 1903 local traveler's guide listed a full complement of passenger trains stopping at Greenville's Erie & Pittsburgh Railroad depot. There were nine trains a day: four to Pittsburgh, three to Jamestown, and two to Erie. On Sundays, there were two trains to Jamestown and two to Pittsburgh. The railroad also advertised special excursion trains to area fairs and expositions.

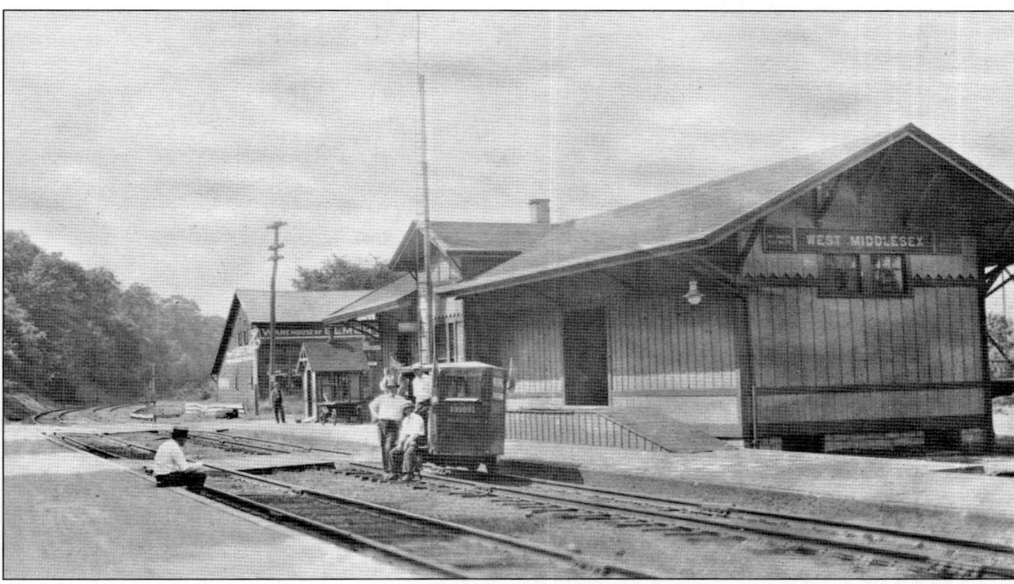

The Erie & Pittsburgh Railroad station at West Middlesex was built in 1872 but burned down in April 1921. The fire was ignited by burglars who blew the lock off the safe, which contained only a few dollars. The depot had been targeted by burglars several times previously that year. It was replaced by three old railroad cars that served as passenger and freight stations.

Hadley and Clarks Mills were stations on the Lake Shore & Michigan Southern Franklin Branch, only three miles apart in the Mercer County countryside, but with quite different facilities in these views. Hadley (above) had a standard-issue Lake Shore & Michigan Southern structure with a semi-detached privy on the front. The station was closed in December 1956 and sold to a private party. It was eventually torn down. Clarks Mills, pictured below in 1919, was outfitted with two retired boxcars for passenger and freight stations. Although these facilities were modest, the station was outfitted with a decorative lamp to illuminate the train schedule board near the front door. (Below, courtesy of Allen County Museum & Historical Society collection.)

In 1886, the narrow-gauge New Brighton & New Castle Railroad purchased the old Matheny Inn, which was built around 1836 along the canal, and turned it into a station for Rock Point Park. The railroad-owned amusement park closed in 1911, and passenger service ended. The old station building was used for a few years as a section house for the Pennsylvania Railroad.

Stoneboro was named for industrialist Amasa Stone, who had coal mining interests in the area and served as director of the LS&MS. Stone's Mercer Iron and Coal Company was a source of significant coal tonnage from the late 1800s until the 1920s. While coal was moving out of the town, summer vacationers were moving in to visit the popular tourist attractions Lake Side Park and the Stoneboro Fair.

The Jamestown Lake Shore & Michigan Southern combination passenger/freight depot dates to 1872. There may have been an earlier station here as the line from Jamestown to Franklin opened on June 27, 1867. After seeing duty as a feed mill post-retirement, the 1872 station served as a woodcarver's gallery from 1995 to 2011. Increased freight business led the railroad to add a dedicated freight station in 1904. A year later, a boxcar body with a platform was added as an additional freight house. In the photograph of the freight station below, the edge of the Jamestown PRR station can be seen at right as the tracks crossed near where the photographer was standing. The wooden planks in the foreground served as a walkway for those transferring railroads to the LS&MS passenger station, which is out of frame to the left.

The Erie & Pittsburgh station at Jamestown was built in 1888 following the loss of the previous depot to fire. After the passenger portion of the station was torn down, passenger operations were consolidated into the freight section. That remaining part of the station was torn down in the mid-1960s shortly after the agency there closed.

The Chewton, Baltimore & Ohio Railroad station was built around 1900 after the Chewton cutoff was completed, replacing the station that was on the old grade. The railroad tried to close it several times, but local businessmen protested. According to news reports, it was closed in 1911, then reopened, then closed again in 1914. It appears to be closed in this 1919 photograph.

The original Pittsburgh & Lake Erie combination passenger and freight station in Ellwood City primarily served the U.S. Steel Shelby Steel Tube Works. As of this 1918 view, the new union station had opened, and this depot then served as a freight-only station. The long platform on the left side of the station extended right up to the steel mill's doors.

Soon after the Pittsburgh & Western built this station at Ellwood City in the early 1890s, one real estate firm rented special passenger cars on trains from Pittsburgh and charged $1 for a round trip for potential buyers to tour what it called "the future summer resort of Western Pennsylvania." The station was replaced with the new brick union station in 1912. (Courtesy of Mark Barnes.)

After years of negotiations between the railroads and the city, the Ellwood City union station opened on October 22, 1912. The station was built by the B&O and Pittsburgh & Lake Erie Railroad railroads on the site of the original B&O station. The railroads also added the subway for Fifth Street, eliminating the grade crossing. Plans for the subway were originally rejected by the city due to the low clearance of the underpass. The city demanded that there be enough clearance so an interurban line could be enticed to choose that route into the city. The smoke in the left background above is from the U.S. Steel Shelby Steel Tube Works factory. The photograph below shows the trackside view with the steel mill to the right. The station was torn down in 1956.

Both the Edenburg P&LE station (above) and the Edenburg Pittsburgh, Youngstown & Ashtabula (later PRR) station (below) were witness to wrecks, accidents, and attempted robberies as were many stations during peak traffic years. The Pittsburgh, Youngstown & Ashtabula station, built in 1880 and extended in 1889, was the site of a notable tragedy in 1930. Although the station closed in the 1920s, it was then used for the storage of gasoline and tools. Two sets of brothers (ages 18–21) broke into the station in February 1930. The police speculated that they intended to steal gas for their car during a return trip to Hillsville from Youngstown. The gas exploded, rocking the entire town. The station and the four brothers all met their demises. Throughout the town's history, the name has been spelled as both "Edenburg" and "Edinburg," with the latter being the more common spelling now.

The mileage sign on the Pittsburgh, Youngstown & Ashtabula station at Hillsville overlooking the Mahoning River indicates that it is 73.5 miles from Harbor (Ashtabula) and 54.5 miles from Pittsburgh. The dual large freight doors on the 1876 station were likely to accommodate mining equipment and explosives for the nearby limestone quarries.

The Pittsburgh & Lake Erie Railroad station at Hillsville was built in 1898 after an explosion destroyed the first station there. The railroad had stored 1,000 pounds of dynamite for nearby stone quarries in the original station, and its explosion injured six people and destroyed a nearby dwelling/store. The blast, started by a lightning strike, was so powerful that it also lifted a freight car off the tracks.

The Lake Shore & Michigan Southern Railroad station at Osgood was shared with the Bessemer & Lake Erie Railroad. The B&LE had two lines here, one on the trestle seen in the background above, and a lower grade that crossed under the LS&MS tracks. B&LE passengers bought their tickets at the station and then used a long wooden sidewalk that took them down the hill to a B&LE waiting shelter, as shown below. Osgood, and nearby Amasa Crossing, boasted one of the busiest railroad crossings in the nation as four rail lines met here. Aside from the B&LE and LS&MS stations at Osgood, Amasa Crossing hosted its own LS&MS station and an Erie Railroad station. There was also a small LS&MS yard near the Osgood station.

A station is shown at Grove City on the 1873 map when the town was known as Pine Grove and the railroad was the Shenango & Allegheny Railroad. That original wood frame station burned down in May 1890 in a fire that claimed 14 businesses, a residence, and the depot. Shown here are views of the second Grove City B&LE passenger station. Above is a valuation photograph from 1919, and below is an inventory photograph from 1943 after the station had been stripped of its umbrella shed and some of its decorative trim. (Below, courtesy of Greenville Railroad Park & Museum.)

The original Bessemer & Lake Erie Railroad freight house at Grove City met a fate similar to the first passenger station there. Seven years after the original passenger station was claimed by fire, the original freight station burned down on August 20, 1897, in a blaze that also claimed the nearby McKay Carriage Works. Shown above is the second freight station in 1919. This station still stands and has been home to Oesterling's Feed and Farm supply store for decades. Aside from fresh coats of paint, the station retains most of its original look, as seen in the 2000 photograph below. (Below, photograph by Steve Heath.)

The Bessemer & Lake Erie Railroad built this extant brick depot at Greenville in 1901. The first Pittsburgh, Shenango & Lake Erie (B&LE predecessor) station here was a two-story brick building on Main Street. The original depot was demolished and replaced with a three-story building that housed B&LE offices. That building also still stands as the Old Town Building at 160 Main Street, as seen here in 2000. (Author photograph.)

The Bessemer & Lake Erie Railroad Fredonia depot was apparently somewhat of a lightning rod. In 1903, the station was struck by lightning but was unharmed. Then, in 1905, the engineer of a passing ore train was struck by lightning. He was unharmed due to the fact that a loose telegraph wire was fortuitously touching the engine and grounded the bolt. (Courtesy of Greenville Railroad Park & Museum.)

The station at Houston Junction was only a mile northeast of Mercer. At the junction with the Western New York & Pennsylvania Railroad, it served the Bessemer and Lake Erie Railroad and its predecessors, from 1859–1919. As the railroad consolidated some operations during World War I, this station and the nearby Mercer B&LE station were closed, and passenger traffic was shifted to the Mercer PRR station.

The Western New York & Pennsylvania station at Mercer, shown in this 1940 view, was on the south side of East Market Street. During World War I, both the PRR and Bessemer & Lake Erie used this station. Thereafter, it became a union depot. (Courtesy of Greenville Railroad Park & Museum.)

New Castle's Erie Railroad station was built in 1887 when the New Castle & Shenango Valley Railroad started this line north to Sharon. The Erie Railroad later intended to build the line all the way down to Pittsburgh, but New Castle was as far as it was built. The station saw only sporadic excursion passenger traffic in the early 1900s until it was remodeled and used by the Pittsburgh & Lake Erie Railroad following the demise of Union Station. The P&LE occupied the station from 1914 until 1933. In 1977, the vacant station was moved and remodeled. Shown below in 2013, now without its distinctive cupola, it currently houses the Lawrence County Chamber of Commerce. (Below, photograph by Wayne Cole.)

The Baltimore & Ohio Railroad's Mill Street freight station in New Castle also housed some railroad offices in its commodious head end (above), and at one time was considered for modification into a temporary passenger station. Over the years, the station saw a brisk freight business with everything from grain to dynamite loaded and unloaded here. Each year from 1919 through at least the mid-1960s, the station received wool from the Lawrence County Cooperative Wool Pool. In 1964, farmers from the surrounding counties loaded 98,454 pounds of wool over two days at the station. The photograph below shows the side of the freight house where the trucks and wagons loaded and unloaded. The whole complex, including the office, freight house, and platforms in the rear, was almost 500 feet in length.

The New Castle Erie & Pittsburgh station was built in 1878 and was on the south side of West Washington Street between South Front Street and the river. It was known as the Westside Pennsylvania Railroad station due to it being on the west bank of the Shenango River. In later years, the station was reduced in size and finally torn down in 1962.

After New Castle's old Union Station was gutted by fire in 1910 and finally razed in 1913, this brick station was built on the same site on the east side of the city by the Pennsylvania Railroad in 1914. The station still stands today and is used as a photography studio. It is seen here in 1999. (Author photograph.)

This was the second Pittsburgh, Youngstown & Ashtabula station at Mahoningtown. It was built in 1877 to replace an earlier structure at the same location. It eventually came to be known as the New Castle Cherry Street Station. Notable trains that drew a crowd when stopping at the station included the Liberty Bell, which toured the PRR in 1915, and the 1940 whistle-stop presidential campaign of Republican candidate Wendell Willkie.

A big celebration and parade kicked off the opening of the new Baltimore & Ohio station at Mahoningtown on June 1, 1917. Nearby streets were strewn with flags and bunting while signs reading "Welcome B&O" were in the windows of businesses. The station was regarded by the railroad and the community as one of the finest on the B&O at the time. It was torn down in the early 1980s.

The original Pittsburgh & Lake Erie Railroad station (above) at Mahoningtown was closed in 1925 but was used as a flag stop thereafter. It was torn down in March 1970. The photograph below shows the newer 1933 P&LE station at center with the Baltimore & Ohio station on the right. There was no agent at the P&LE station, so it was more of a fancy waiting room and platform than a full-blown station. The P&LE ticket agent was actually in an office in downtown New Castle with bus shuttle service to Mahoningtown. The Baltimore & Ohio agent also handled P&LE tickets and freight from that station, so this became a sort of union station complex. (Below, photograph by John W. Barriger III, courtesy of Barriger National Railroad Library at University of Missouri St. Louis.)

This joint freight station at New Castle was shared by the Pittsburgh & Lake Erie Railroad and the Erie Railroad. It was built in 1913 and opened in January 1914. The station still stands at Grove and Neal Streets and now houses a Consolidated Container factory. The freight house portion is now unrecognizable, but the head office end retains the same look as in this 1916 view.

Lawrence Junction was just south of Mahoningtown near the confluence of the Shenango and Beaver Rivers. It was here that several Pennsylvania Railroad predecessor lines met, including the main lines of the Erie & Pittsburgh Railroad and the Pittsburgh, Youngstown & Ashtabula Railroad. This photograph shows two of the passenger waiting shelters. Tickets were likely sold from a nearby station building.

New Castle Junction was just across the Shenango River to the southeast of Lawrence Junction. It was a major facility on the Baltimore & Ohio and Pittsburgh & Lake Erie Railroads. Both lines had roundhouses at the junction, and during its heyday, over 500 workers were employed there. The photographs above and below are from Pittsburgh & Lake Erie Railroad valuation records from 1919. The images show the passenger station and umbrella shed. The station was built in 1895, and two long new umbrella sheds—one 240 feet and one 560 feet—were added around 1906. The B&O roundhouse burned down in 1975, but the P&LE roundhouse still stands and is used by Kasgro Rail Corporation, a builder of railroad cars and fleet management firm.

The Gardner Avenue Pittsburgh & Lake Erie Railroad station on the south side of New Castle opened in 1907. The Baltimore & Ohio Railroad, which ran parallel to the P&LE here, also had passenger service at the station. The station was built primarily to serve the American Tin Plate Company rolling mill. The station was closed in the early 1930s.

The oddly shaped Pittsburgh, Youngstown & Ashtabula Railroad station at Wampum Junction is shown in this c. 1916 view. At Wampum Junction, the lower-grade line left the high line on the west side of the Beaver River and crossed over to the east side. This was a busy junction as trains from Erie to Pittsburgh crossed over here, as well as trains running from Pittsburgh to Cleveland.

The Pittsburgh & Lake Erie Railroad station at Wampum afforded passengers eight westbound and seven eastbound trains per day in the early 1900s. Residents, however, were displeased because the late train from New Castle returned them too early, so they missed out on nighttime entertainment in that city. A newspaper item from 1914 conveyed their wishes to travel by streetcar instead. The passenger station closed in 1964 and was torn down not long after. The freight station, shown below around 1916, still stands and was renovated in 2015 as a community center. The property also provides access to the North Country Scenic Trail.

The Moravia Pittsburgh & Lake Erie Railroad combination passenger/freight station was built in 1892 but moved to West Pittsburg in 1900 to serve as the station there. At the time, West Pittsburg was growing faster than Moravia. Just eight years later, a larger brick station was added at West Pittsburg, so the old Moravia station thereafter served as the freight station.

The Pittsburgh & Lake Erie Railroad station at West Pittsburg opened on May 1, 1908, and was followed by the opening of a new quadruple-tracked section of mainline later that year that started just north of the station and ran to Mahoningtown. The station still stands and is slated for renovation by the Beaver Lawrence Railway Historical Society. The nonprofit group also owns an interlocking tower, watchman's shanty, and several rail cars.

Three

Venango and Forest Counties

Venango County was the heart of the Pennsylvania oil boom, which meant a railroad boom as well during the late 1800s. Sparsely populated Forest County was home to logging railroads that provided lumber for railroad construction in the area. The Allegheny Valley Railroad (later PRR) bed running north-south through Venango County has been repurposed to host a network of connected bicycle trails, including a popular 27-mile section of the Allegheny River Trail between Franklin and Emlenton.

This classic Atlantic & Great Western depot at Utica, between Cochranton and Franklin, was built in 1875. The station area featured a 50,000-gallon water tank that was filled from the adjacent French Creek. At some point, the station's size was greatly reduced, and the remaining portion was purchased by a private party. The remainder of the station, shown below in 2015, has been restored and is now used as a seasonal cabin on the bank of French Creek not far from its original location. Although much smaller now, the station still retains some of its distinctive architecture. (Below, photograph by Steve Heath.)

During the time that Raymilton was the western terminus of the line from Oil City, it was a coal-producing hub for refineries, but it was soon surpassed in coal production by Stoneboro when the line was extended westward. However, profitable oil wells sprung up along the line and replaced coal as the town's main export. Aside from the station, which was gone by the 1940s, the LS&MS also had an old frame roundhouse and repair shops here.

At Reno, the Atlantic & Great Western Railroad line passed through the Empire Oil Refinery (later Wolf's Head), and this sturdy brick station served that industry. After the station was closed by the railroad, it was used by the refinery and given the inglorious moniker Building No. 10. The station still stands, although the roof has been reduced and flattened, thus stripping it of its distinctive depot profile.

The Lake Shore & Michigan Southern Railroad station at Reno was built in 1871 according to the standard plans that the line used for many stations throughout Northwest Pennsylvania and Northern Ohio. The station was a combination passenger and freight depot that measured 20 feet by 102 feet. Nearby stations at Raymilton and Polk looked similar but were about half as long.

A once busy station on the Allegheny Valley Railroad between Oil City and Pittsburgh, Kennerdell was cut off from the mainline with the installation of the Kennerdell Tunnel in 1915. In addition to the Woodhill and East Brady tunnels, these shortcuts shaved 15 miles of trackage off the mainline. After that, Kennerdell saw only a few local trains until service ended, and the tracks were removed in 1930.

Franklin's new Lake Shore & Michigan Southern passenger station opened on September 14, 1901, with a reception for journalists, citizens, and railroad officials, who heralded it as one of the finest on the line. It was built to similar specifications as a number of stations on the Lakefront line of that era, such as North East, Pennsylvania, and Geneva and Conneaut, Ohio. It is seen above in 1919. The station still stands and is used as a child-care center. The freight station, pictured below in 1919, dates to 1867. The two-story head house section still stands, although its appearance has been heavily modified following a 2001 fire that claimed the one-story rear section. (Above, courtesy of Allen County Museum & Historical Society collection.)

Franklin's Allegheny Valley Railroad station was across the Allegheny River from Franklin on the east bank, so access required crossing the Eighth Street bridge on the south end of the city. Because the station was about a mile from the center of town, parades led by the high school band were common when the Pennsylvania National Guard Company L, 112th Infantry boarded troop trains during World War I and World War II. After passenger service ended, the station was converted to freight only and appears to have been shortened somewhat, as evidenced in the view below from 1960. (Below, photograph by Ed Weber III.)

The Emlenton Allegheny Valley Railroad passenger depot originally served as the station at Fullerton, which was just south of Emlenton, where Ritchie Run empties into the Allegheny River. Sometime prior to 1900, the station was cut into two sections and moved from Fullerton north to Emlenton. On February 25, 1961, eighteen cars in the middle of a 78-car Pennsylvania Railroad coal train derailed at the station and piled up in an area about 50 yards in length. Three of the cars hit the station, causing heavy damage to the structure. Soon after, the station was torn down. During the demolition, workers found Allegheny Valley Railroad documents dating to 1876. The spartan freight station, which sat across the tracks from the passenger station, is shown below.

The Rouseville Pennsylvania Railroad depot is shown here in March 1962, almost 100 years after the first station was opened here on the Farmers Railroad (later part of the PRR) in 1866. Like many other towns along Oil Creek, the oil boom came and went, and the station and oil tanks in the photograph are now gone. (Photograph by Ed Weber III.)

Built by the Western New York & Pennsylvania Railroad, this brick union station at Oil City was also used by the Erie Railroad. It opened in 1883. The station and two nearby freight houses were burned down in a July 1962 ceremony by the city to make way for a new development project on the site. This image was captured on March 3, 1962. (Photograph Ed Weber III.)

Miller Farm, on the Western New York & Pennsylvania, was notable for being the terminus of the first pipeline built in the United States. The pipeline ran from the oil wells at Pithole five miles to Miller Farm, where the oil was transferred to barrels and, later, tanker cars for shipment via the railroad. Miller Farm had a more significant railroad station at first than the structure shown in this 1917 photograph. The original station burned down on May 8, 1901. The night trackwalker and his wife lived in the station at the time. Although the trackwalker was out on rounds when the fire started, their barking dog alerted his wife to the fire, and she was able to escape unharmed, but the depot was consumed. Although the name "Miller Farm" and the small station suggests a small town, the town that sprung up around Miller Farm at one time boasted 11 hotels, iron storage tanks, loading racks, and other oil facilities.

The Franklin & Clearfield Railroad station at Van was built in 1909 when the line opened. A June 17, 1911, article in the *Franklin News-Herald* said that the station provided opportunities for people in nearby Pinegrove Township to travel to Franklin to shop after they had previously gone to Oil City for that purpose. This picture was taken in 1919. (Courtesy of Allen County Museum & Historical Society collection.)

The Baltimore & Ohio Railroad station at Marienville dates from 1905. The previous Pittsburgh & Western Railroad station was destroyed by a 1902 fire that left 500 residents homeless and destroyed most buildings in town. So great was the destruction that consideration was given to not rebuilding the town at all. The town was rebuilt, and the Marienville depot was resurrected as a passenger station from 1986 to 2006 for Knox & Kane Railroad tourist excursions.

Here are two examples of stations that also served as dwellings for the railroad agent, trackwalker, or section chief. Dotter station (above) on the Allegheny Valley Railroad was built in 1903 and looked like a standard house. The lamppost and station sign in front gives away its purpose. Sugar Creek station on the Atlantic & Great Western Railroad was built in 1875–1876, according to railroad valuation records. A larger structure with a more railroad-building look, it nonetheless had living quarters on the second floor. According to the *Franklin News-Herald*, the station was razed on June 20, 1933, and the lumber was salvaged by a man who planned to build a house with it in Maple Dale.

Because of its central role in the oil export business, Oil City warranted the construction of large passenger and freight stations by the Lake Shore & Michigan Southern Railroad. The passenger station is shown above. Below, the 126-foot-long freight station can be seen with a platform full of incoming oil well equipment. Both stations were built in 1870–1871, when the railroad was known as the Jamestown and Franklin Railroad. The stations were demolished in 1966 to make way for US Highway 62. Both photographs were taken around 1919 for Interstate Commerce Commission valuation records that documented all property owned by US railroads.

Four

Clarion and Jefferson Counties

The two major railroad players in Clarion and Jefferson Counties were the Pittsburgh & Western, which crossed Clarion County diagonally, and the Allegheny Valley Railroad Low Grade Division, which began in Clarion County and bisects Jefferson County. A later arrival to the area was the New York Central's Franklin and Clearfield Branch that was completed in 1911. It crossed Clarion County and terminated at Rose Siding in Jefferson County. The Buffalo, Rochester & Pittsburgh Railroad (BR&P, later B&O) also traversed the east side of Jefferson County.

The station at Knox appears to be a standard Baltimore & Ohio Railroad station with a freight house attached. A closer look at the back of the building in the 1920 view below, though, reveals that the railroad had also attached a residence to the depot, presumably for the station agent. The passenger section and residence are gone, but the freight section still stands as of 2019 (in poor condition). This line through Knox began as the narrow-gauge P&W and was converted to standard gauge by the B&O. It served as a tourist line as the Knox & Kane Railroad until 2006.

Bryners Station was on the Pittsburgh & Western Railroad about a mile south of Shippenville. There was a mill here and not much else. Today, a back road dead-ends near where the station used to be, and there are no houses nearby. In this c. 1917 view, a section foreman seems to be supervising the repair or dismantling of the incomplete, and seemingly impromptu, passenger and freight shelter.

Reidsburg went through a small oil rush in the 1880s, but by the time the Jamestown, Franklin & Clearfield Railroad built through this area of central Clarion County, the town of about 20 dwellings and a few shops only warranted a converted boxcar as a station. The first wells drilled here did not yield much, and hopes of an oil boom faded.

Shippenville's station (above) on the Franklin & Clearfield Railroad was built in 1909 but lasted only 26 years before a blaze sparked by a faulty chimney flue claimed it in 1935. Within hours of the station burning down, Stationmaster D.I. Pfaff, who received burns to his arm saving records and equipment from the blaze, had set up shop in the tool house pictured to the right of the station above. Instead of replacing the depot with another permanent structure, the railroad used a converted passenger car body. That car body station is shown below in the 1950s after passenger service had ended. (Below, photograph by John W. Barriger III, courtesy of Barriger National Railroad Library at the University of Missouri St. Louis.)

The Shippenville Pittsburgh & Western station served for a much longer tenure than the Shippenville station on the Franklin & Clearfield Railroad. The P&W line was originally opened as the narrow-gauge Emlenton & Shippenville Railroad in 1875, primarily serving oil wells and sawmills along its route. The station's classic B&O-style profile means it was likely built in the 1890s.

This postcard shows the Pittsburgh, Summerville & Clarion Railroad station at Clarion. The PS&C was a precursor to the Lake Erie, Franklin & Clarion (LEF&C). This was the original wood-frame station, which was on the east side of Ninth Avenue between Wood and Main Streets. The station burned down in 1910 and was replaced with a single-story brick station.

Limestone on the Jamestown, Franklin & Clearfield Railroad served for only two years before it was consumed by a lightning-sparked blaze in the summer of 1911. Pictured here is the replacement that was erected in 1912. It is likely an exact duplicate of the first station and built to the same plans as the other stations along this line from that era, including Van, Shippenville, and Elmo.

The Jamestown, Franklin & Clearfield Railroad station at Elmo was constructed in 1909 when the railroad was built to connect the New York Central's lines west of Buffalo with the Clearfield coal district, where the railroad already had a presence with several smaller lines. At the time, Elmo was only a collection of a few dairy farms, as it is today.

The schedule board on the Jamestown, Franklin & Clearfield Railroad station at Sutton lists only one eastbound and one westbound train for the day. This station was smaller than the others along the line due to its isolated location, which is inaccessible by road today. It only served as a station from 1909 to 1919 and thereafter was simply a train order office.

Red Bank station was near the junction point on the Buffalo & Allegheny Valley Division of the Pennsylvania Railroad, where the low-grade branch met the two-track mainline at the mouth of Red Bank Creek. Pictured is the third station built here after the first two burned down. This station would meet the same fate in 1945, and the railroad replaced it with a brick structure that stood until the 1980s.

The Allegheny Valley Railroad was built along the bank of the Allegheny River during the years 1866–1867. The combination passenger and freight station at West Monterey was of standard design and was the second one at West Monterey after the first burned down in 1899. Compare the design of this station with the one at Kennerdell in Venango County and Parkers Landing below.

Parkers Landing was also known as Parkers Station and East Parker. The original Allegheny Valley Railroad station was just north of where the old Parker & Karns City Railroad bridge crossed the river. Parker City, which was on the west bank of the river, was served by the B&O, and that station is pictured on page 114.

The Allegheny Valley Railroad station at East Brady overlooked the Allegheny River and sat just north of the bridge that spanned the river between East Brady and Bradys Bend in Armstrong County. The c. 1915 photograph above shows the station as a busy hub of passenger and freight activity when this section of track was part of the mainline. In 1916, the towns of East Brady and Phillipston were bypassed due to the construction of the Brady Tunnel. The photograph below taken on July 14, 1957, shows that the station has been shortened and was probably only used for infrequent freight service by that time, as the line through town was part of the East Brady Branch of the Pennsylvania Railroad. (Below, photograph by Ed Weber III.)

Kingsville's Jamestown, Franklin & Clearfield Railroad passenger shelter, built in 1914, featured a partially enclosed front to protect waiting passengers from the elements and small side windows from which to watch for approaching trains. Kingsville also had a small freight station that was owned by local residents and leased by the railroad. The shelter at Kline (below) had a few more Craftsman flourishes on its trim but offered even less protection from the elements than the shelter at Kingsville. Kline also had a similar-sized section man's shanty and a telephone booth for railroad use about a mile from the passenger shelter. Both of these images were captured in 1919. (Both, courtesy of Allen County Museum & Historical Society collection.)

The Allegheny Valley passenger (above) and freight (below) stations in Foxburg were substantial brick structures with similar architectural flourishes that were built in 1885. Note the recessed pentagon designs on the ends of both buildings. The line officially became a part of the Buffalo and Allegheny Division of the Pennsylvania Railroad in 1910. Passenger traffic on the line through Foxburg ceased around 1950, and the passenger station was demolished by the spring of 1952. The passenger station survived catching fire multiple times during a large blaze in April 1900 that consumed most businesses between the railroad tracks and the river. Railroad employees and volunteers were credited with saving the station that day.

Foxburg's first Pittsburg & Western Railroad station was built in 1883 and destroyed by fire in 1915. The station pictured replaced it soon after. This station had been vacant for years when it, too, finally succumbed to fire in 1975. No trains on the B&O had gone through Foxburg after 1964, and the line was removed in 1982.

In the days of steam engines, hot cinders landing on depot roofs were the cause of numerous fires. The Pittsburgh & Western Railroad station at St. Petersburg was outfitted with a tin roof in an attempt to mitigate that risk. The original railroad through here was the narrow-gauge Foxburg, St. Petersburg & Turkey City Railroad, which was built in the 1870s.

Five

Warren, McKean, and Elk Counties

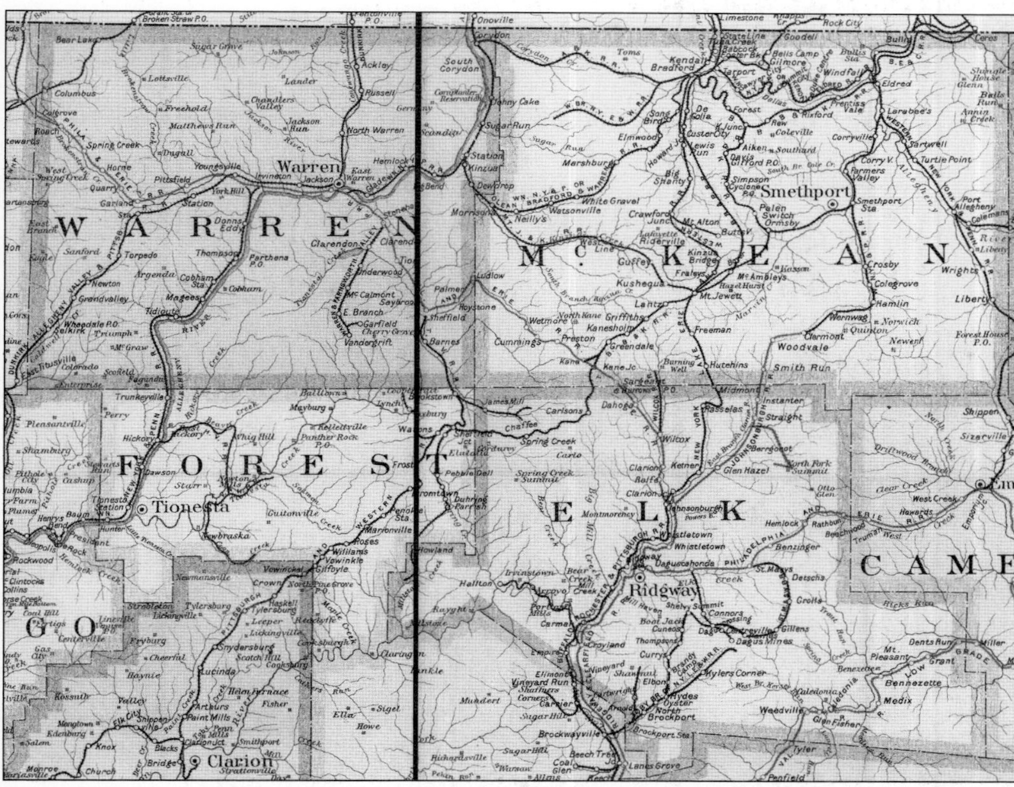

A quick glance at this map shows a tangle of railroads across the tri-county area of Warren, McKean, and Elk. Scores of smaller railroads—and later, leases, mergers, and acquisitions—in the region gave a prominent position to familiar lines Pennsylvania Railroad, Erie Railroad, and New York Central Railroad. Second-tier lines like the Buffalo, Rochester & Pittsburgh and the Pittsburg & Shawmut also played an important role with passenger and freight operations.

The Western New York & Pennsylvania station at Bullis Mill appears to be shuttered in this c. 1919 view. The town's chief industry in the early 1900s was the manufacture of high explosives at the Eldred Powder Company, so the shutters may have been a glass-saving measure. This was the last station in Pennsylvania on the WNY&P before the line crossed over into New York.

Colza station on the Philadelphia & Erie Railroad was two miles from Corry just over the county line in Warren County. The station was built in 1878 to serve local farms. Ernest Miller, in a 1974 article about Warren County place names in the journal *Western Pennsylvania History*, claimed that the name "Colza" was imparted by a Serbian farmer from the Serbian-Croatian word *koza* for "goat."

The Philadelphia & Erie Railroad station at Sheffield, pictured above in 2010, was built in 1880 to replace a smaller wood frame station that was not large enough to handle passenger and freight traffic from the bustling local tannery. The station also served the Sheffield & Tionesta Railroad until that line built its own station (shown in the background above) in 1907. A separate freight house (below) was added in 1907 by the PRR, but it was closed in 1932 as freight traffic waned. Thereafter, freight service was again consolidated into the brick station. The freight station is now gone, but the two brick stations remain and are now museums. (Above, photograph by Jim Cook.)

The Philadelphia & Erie Railroad station at Clarendon had a false start during construction in 1881 when the foundation gave way and the partially built depot collapsed. It was promptly rebuilt more sturdily and served for many years. When a fire gutted the town in 1887 and burned more than 100 buildings, the station was one of very few to be saved, although it did sustain some damage.

The Daguscahonda station, built in 1883, on the Philadelphia & Erie Railroad, was near the junction with the six-mile Daguscahonda Railroad. The Daguscahonda Railroad was built in 1866 to transport coal from the Dagus Mines north to the connection with the P&E. Although the railroad primarily hauled coal, a passenger coach was attached to some trains so passengers could also connect to the east-west P&E line.

Johnsonburg was served by three railroads, with the Philadelphia & Erie having the largest and most central presence in town, while the Buffalo, Rochester & Pittsburgh Railroad and Erie Railroad provided passenger and freight stations, respectively. The brick PRR passenger station (above), built around 1900, was the third PRR station in Johnsonburg, replacing two previous wood-frame union stations that served both the PRR and Erie Railroad. The PRR freight station (below) was just north of where the PRR's Johnsonburg Branch diverged from the mainline heading north to Clermont in Warren County. The freight station was over 100 feet long, owing its size to the considerable paper and brick industries in town. The Johnsonburg Branch was established primarily to haul coal and lumber.

The Philadelphia & Erie Railroad reached Kane in 1864. The station pictured above was built in 1871. The building in the background to the left was the Western Union telegraph office. This station burned down in 1873, as did a temporary depot on May 10, 1874, along with a nearby hotel and outbuildings. Later in 1874, the larger brick passenger station shown below was built along with a nearby freight station. The passenger station still stands and has been renovated to house a museum operated by the Kane Historic Preservation Society. (Above, courtesy of L. Tom Perry Special Collections, Harold B. Lee Library, Brigham Young University.)

The Pennsylvania Railroad station at Irvineton is shown above in busier times around 1919 and below on November 21, 1961, after passenger service had ended and the building was no longer maintained. In 1866, passengers traveling from Philadelphia to then-booming Oil City made the 22-hour trip with a one-hour layover at Irvineton for breakfast before the last leg of the journey. In 1886, the original wood-frame station at Irvineton burned down and was replaced with the brick station shown. At the time, the station was served by the Philadelphia & Erie Railroad and the Western New York & Pennsylvania Railway. Both lines would become part of the Pennsylvania Railroad. (Below, photograph by Ed Weber III.)

Shown above is the first New York & Lake Erie Railroad (later Erie Railroad) passenger station at Bradford. It was also used by the Western New York & Pennsylvania and the narrow-gauge Bradford, Bordell, and Kinzua. After it went out of service when the new Erie station was built, it was demolished in the middle of the night by the railroad in 1891 by being dragged down by cables attached to a locomotive. The newer 1890 Erie station is shown below. The Bradford Board of Commerce moved its offices into the second floor in 1941, and passenger service ended in 1949. The station suffered two fires in 1953 and was demolished in 1954 to facilitate a street extension project. (Below, courtesy of Steamtown National Historic Site Erie Railroad plate glass negative collection.)

East Bradford station, also known as Tarport, on the Erie Railroad, sat quite close to an old oil derrick. Such was the promise of oil in the area that wells were often close to buildings and sometimes drilled in the middle of streets. The station was razed in October 1938 to enhance driver visibility on the street. (Courtesy of Steamtown National Historic Site.)

The Erie Railroad depot at Columbus looks as if a freight train has collided with the building, but it is actually two boxcars repurposed as a freight house. Using boxcars for stations was common on the Erie Railroad. This was the third station at Columbus and was built in 1908. (Courtesy of Steamtown National Historic Site Erie Railroad plate glass negative collection.)

Pictured is the Tidioute Western Pennsylvania & New York Railroad (later PRR) station about 10 years before it was torn down. A freight station and the Tidioute Refining Company, built in 1919, were just south of the passenger station. The station was razed around 1970 to make room for a parking lot. This photograph was taken on November 21, 1961. (Photograph by Ed Weber III.)

Some railroad employees appear to be having a confab outside the overgrown Garland Philadelphia & Erie Railroad depot in this August 1960 view. The station was built in 1887. A 1929 nostalgia piece in the *Warren Times-Mirror* recollected that the evening train from Corry on Saturday nights would stop at Garland and "unload drunks like a lot of mailbags." This image was captured on August 18, 1960. (Photograph by Ed Weber III.)

Part of the Erie Railroad's Bradford Branch was comprised of the former Buffalo, Bradford & Pittsburgh Railroad that ran from Carrollton, New York, to Gilesville, Pennsylvania. The branch was extended in 1882 to reach Johnsonburg. The line was also used by the Buffalo, Rochester & Pittsburgh due to long-term leased trackage rights from the Erie Railroad from J&B Junction, just north of Mt. Jewett, to Clarion Junction, which was just north of Johnsonburg. Shown above is the Erie Railroad station at Hutchins, and below is the BR&P Hutchins station. This was a unique example of one town having two stations of different railroads on one line. (Above, courtesy of Steamtown National Historic Site Erie Railroad plate glass negative collection.)

Rasselas, on the Erie Railroad's Bradford Branch, saw its fair share of railroad accidents over the years. In 1883, two coal trains collided. Unfortunately, there was a passenger car attached to the rear of the first train, and six lives were lost. Auto accidents were common here too as the line crosses Rasselas Road three times in the span of 1.3 miles.

Mt. Jewett on the Erie Railroad's Bradford Branch also served the BR&P. Formerly known as Howard Hill, the town was renamed in honor of Hugh Judge Jewett, a former US representative from Ohio who served as president of the Erie Railroad from 1874 to 1884. The station was shortened in 1958 after a freight train derailed into the freight house end of the building.

The Philadelphia & Erie Railroad station at Warren was built in 1868. It originally had a cupola in the center of the roof, but that was removed around 1900. The station was listed in the National Register of Historic Places in 1974 but was torn down by Conrail in 1986 at the borough's request when a private buyer could not be found. This photograph was taken on November 21, 1961. (Photograph by Ed Weber III.)

The Dunkirk, Allegheny Valley & Pittsburgh at North Warren saw its last regular passenger train in 1937. The railroad, nicknamed the "Dolly Varden," made the last run from Dunkirk, New York, to Titusville, Pennsylvania. The station is seen here in 2000 when it was a pizza shop. It has since been converted into a diner called The Train Station. (Photograph by Steve Heath.)

The Philadelphia & Erie Railroad station at St. Marys was built in 1881, succeeding the previous stations here that burned down in 1872 and 1880. The station was also used by the Pittsburg, Shawmut & Northern Railroad after that line's station went out of service. It was torn down in 1972 to make way for the Depot Street municipal parking lot. This image was captured on October 3, 1971. (Photograph by Ed Weber III.)

The Philadelphia & Erie freight station at Wilcox appears to stand alone in the wilderness in this 1964 photograph. However, during the boom years of Wilcox, the freight station and its companion passenger station (gone by the time the photograph was taken on August 4, 1964) were busy places serving the lumber, oil, and tanning industry there. (Photograph by Ed Weber III.)

Ridgway is a great destination for railroad buffs as the borough has two restored brick stations. On the west side of the Clarion River is the 1905 Buffalo, Rochester & Pittsburgh Railroad station (above in 2000). The 1907 colonial revival-style Philadelphia & Erie station (seen below on August 21, 1972) is on the east side of the river. The P&E station was one of the last built by that line before it was formally merged with the Pennsylvania Railroad. Ridgway, which was once home to a railroad car and snowplow manufacturer, boasts a historic district that was listed in the National Register of Historic Places in 2003. (Above, author photograph; below, photograph by Ed Weber III.)

The Smethport Pittsburg Shawmut & Northern Railroad station was a relatively late addition for a passenger station, having been built in 1928. As the other railroads in Smethport were winding down passenger service and tearing down stations, the Shawmut invested $15,000 in this stucco and tile station. Seen here in 2000, it still stands and is used as a business. (Author photograph.)

The busy Western New York & Pennsylvania Railroad station at Eldred is seen in a postcard view from the early 1900s. By 1966, the station had lost its agent and only had flag-stop service and a part-time freight agent who traveled from Port Allegany a few times per week. Although the station is gone, the railroad was resurrected in 2001 as a new version of the WNY&P.

Six

Butler and Armstrong Counties

Butler and Armstrong Counties, and the rail lines that served the area, fed off the mainstays of Western Pennsylvania industrial heritage—steel, coal, and oil—as well as some pottery works. The centrally located cities of Butler and Kittanning were part of the steel belt. Butler was served by the Bessemer & Lake Erie, Pittsburg & Western, and Western Penn Railroads. Kittanning was served by the Pennsylvania and Pittsburg & Shawmut Railroads.

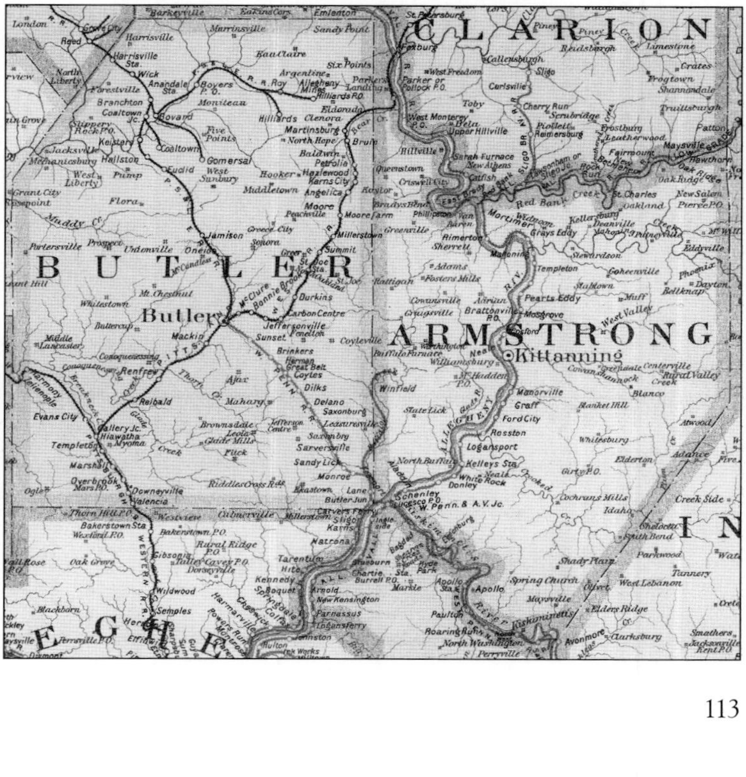

Parkers Landing started off as a small village of less than 1,000 until an oil boom swept the area, sending the population soaring to around 20,000 with the new moniker Parker City. The standard B&O station pictured here was likely built in the early 1900s, by which time the population was back to under 1,000 residents. The village is now known as the "smallest city in the USA."

Once a busy railroad town at the junction of two B&O subdivisions, Callery Junction had three generations of stations. The first burned down in 1892 when the town was almost wiped off the map by a village-wide blaze. The second station burned down in 1917. The third, pictured here in 1919 and still standing today, was a converted residence or hotel with the tracks running in front of the building.

Originally known as Barnhart's Mills, and then Millerstown, the local post office and Pittsburgh & Western Railroad changed the names of the post office and station to Chicora in 1891. Townsfolk were split on the name change, and the name "Chicora" was not officially adopted by the borough council until 1959. Although the origin is not known for sure, it was likely named after a town in South Carolina.

In this c. 1918 view of the P&W station at Bruin, it appears that a roof replacement project is almost finished to ensure that stray embers from passing trains do not set the depot alight. The railroad, which ran along Bear Creek, also served the High Grade Oil Refinery in Bruin with the installation of a 40-car siding at the plant in 1911.

The Pittsburgh & Western passenger (above) and freight (below) stations in Butler were built in the early 1880s. By the early 1900s, the town had grown, as had railroad traffic, as evidenced by the busy scene above. In 1911, about 50 prominent businesses and industrial interests petitioned the railroads to join together to erect a new union station. Their efforts were futile, however, and the P&W instead kept expanding the stations with additions. During their years of service, both stations expanded to twice their original lengths. The passenger station started as a one-story building, but a two-story office and lunchroom were added. The freight station doubled from 100 feet to 200 feet in the 1910s. After the Bessemer & Lake Erie closed its station in Butler, it moved its passenger operations into the B&O station, and the town finally had a union station of sorts.

Petrolia was an oil boomtown in the late 1800s, and with oil wells in close proximity to dwellings and businesses, it suffered frequent fires. The worst was a Fourth of July 1893 blaze that claimed most of the town save for one hotel and the Pittsburgh & Western station pictured here. A flood in 1879 that swept most of the town's business district downstream also spared the depot.

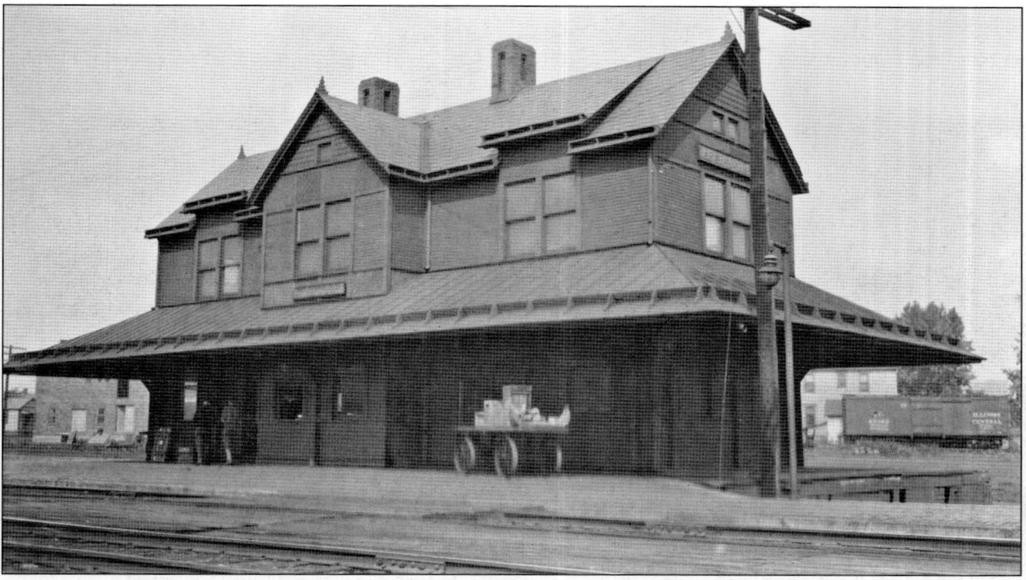

Zelienople's two-story station was erected in 1897 by the P&W, replacing the original station, which was opened in 1879 when the line was known as the Pittsburgh, New Castle & Lake Erie. In its first annual report, the line touted shipping 9,570 pounds of butter and 8,000 dozen eggs in one day.

At first glance, the Baltimore & Ohio Railroad station (above) at Evans City looks unremarkable save for the decorative rounded ends. A look at the photograph below, however, shows that this station was one of a kind. The depot was built in 1909 and was supposedly noted by *Ripley's Believe It Or Not!* to be the only railroad station in the world to be constructed over water. Part of this platform, which spans Breakneck Creek right in the middle of town, remained as of 2020. In the early years, one drawback of having the station over the creek was that the town's sewage system emptied into the creek nearby, which created unwelcome odors during the summer. The station was demolished by the railroad around 1980.

The Pittsburgh & Western station at Renfrew is shown around 1917. The B&O closed the station in January 1915 due to dwindling business, but protests from citizens made the railroad reopen it in April 1915. Upon reopening, the railroad asked the citizens to "co-operate with us to increase freight and passenger traffic," according to the *Butler Citizen* on April 1, 1915.

The P&W station at Mars is a success story of community restoration efforts. The station was moved from trackside in 1999 and has been meticulously restored in the intervening years. The building, seen here in 2020, now houses the Mars Area History and Landmarks Society, and the site includes a caboose and a trolley station as part of the attraction. (Photograph by Matt Cesare.)

The Bessemer & Lake Erie Railroad passenger station at Butler was a converted hotel rather than a conventional depot building. The station occupied the two buildings on the left in the above 1932 photograph. The station was closed in 1914 when the railroad laid a crossover track to access the parallel Baltimore & Ohio tracks and station for passenger service instead. After going out of service, the old station retained its signage and was used for railroad offices. According to the *Butler Citizen*, 45 soldiers from Company C of the 18th Pennsylvania Infantry were housed in the old station awaiting active duty during World War I. The B&LE freight house, shown below in 1955, was just east of downtown off Kittanning Street. (Both, courtesy of the Greenville Railroad Park & Museum.)

Euclid, on the Shenango & Allegheny Railroad, was named by the railroad in 1882. The station served the nearby town of Sunbury (now West Sunbury). Upon the line's completion, editors at the *Butler Citizen* bemoaned several of the names given to places on this line by the railroad as some names had no local connection to the towns they served, Euclid included.

Although Branchton was a small town, it had a large Bessemer & Lake Erie Railroad station due to the fact that the 10-mile Hilliards Branch diverged from the mainline here. That branch line was the source of significant coal and limestone production, so by 1910, Branchton also had a yard with a capacity of 1,000 cars for assembling trains to journey north or south on the mainline.

Queen Junction appeared virtually overnight on the Bessemer & Lake Erie Railroad when the Western Allegheny Railroad formed the junction in 1906. The station served both railroads and saw brisk passenger business in the early days. By the time this photograph was taken in 1941, part of the Western Allegheny had been abandoned, and passenger traffic on the B&LE had dwindled to new lows. (Courtesy of Greenville Railroad Park & Museum.)

The sparsely populated area around Cunningham near the Butler/Allegheny County line on the Bessemer & Lake Erie Railroad barely warranted a station. The railroad erected this passenger waiting shed there from standard plans that were typically used to build tool storage sheds. Although the shelter and stove provided some respite from the weather, the station had no electricity or plumbing.

Hallston, also known as Pump, was a small station on the Bessemer & Lake Erie Railroad. The station is on the right; the building on the left was used as a tool house and track crew sleeping quarters. According to a 1913 article in the *Butler Citizen*, it was at this building that detectives made their first arrest in stopping a string of petty robberies along the line.

There were only a few buildings at Keisters on the Bessemer & Lake Erie Railroad, but the location warranted a much larger station than at Hallston. This was due to the station serving as the main arrival and departure point for students at Slippery Rock State Normal School (now Slippery Rock University). A hack line carried passengers and mail over the four miles from the station to the college.

According to Bessemer & Lake Erie records, this station at West Saxonburg was built at Odell in 1905 and moved in 1911 to West Saxonburg, where it was remodeled. A second station at Odell was also moved to West Saxonburg, where it was converted into a house for railroad employees. This photograph is from around 1917.

The Allegheny Valley Railroad station at Rimerton was built in 1913. This station is evidence that railroads would even locate stations in very small towns. At the time of its construction, Rimerton consisted only of 12 houses, a hotel, and two stores. Today, not much more than that remains at Rimerton. The station was torn down sometime during World War II.

White Rock station on the mainline of the Allegheny Valley Railroad was on the east bank of the Allegheny River. It was one of a number of stations along the line that served small river communities between Schenley and Ford City. A nearby ferry transported passengers, animals, and freight across the river. This image is from 1910. (Photograph by John P. Klingensmith, courtesy of the Leechburg Area Museum & Historical Society.)

The Kittanning Pittsburg & Shawmut Railroad station is on the west bank of the Allegheny River in the Applewold section of town. It was built in 1913 and modeled in the same general shape as the Pennsylvania Railroad station in Kittanning (see the following page). The passenger station and a nearby freight station are still used by the Buffalo & Pittsburgh Railroad. This photograph was taken in 2000. (Author photograph.)

The Kittanning Pennsylvania Railroad passenger station (shown above around 1999) and freight station (below) were built in 1895 at a cost of $20,000 to replace two wood-frame stations at approximately the same location. The freight station is a unique terminal-type station where up to six freight cars could be pulled into the station and several more alongside it. In the photograph of the freight station, it appears that an outgoing shipment of cases of beer is being unloaded onto the platform by a man driving a Kittanning Brewing Company truck. Both stations still exist. (Above, author photograph.)

INDEX OF PHOTOGRAPHS

Discover Thousands of Local History Books Featuring Millions of Vintage Images

Arcadia Publishing, the leading local history publisher in the United States, is committed to making history accessible and meaningful through publishing books that celebrate and preserve the heritage of America's people and places.

Find more books like this at
www.arcadiapublishing.com

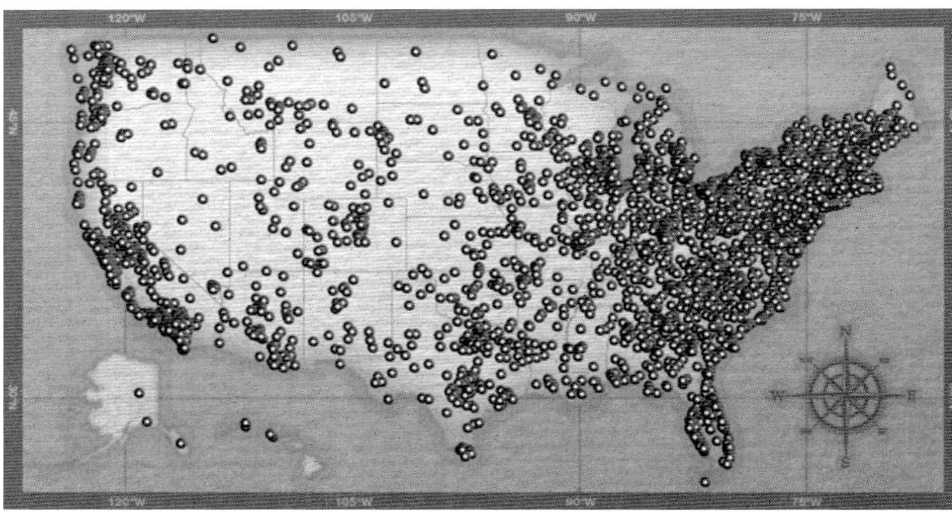

Search for your hometown history, your old stomping grounds, and even your favorite sports team.

Consistent with our mission to preserve history on a local level, this book was printed in South Carolina on American-made paper and manufactured entirely in the United States. Products carrying the accredited Forest Stewardship Council (FSC) label are printed on 100 percent FSC-certified paper.

MADE IN THE USA